# God I need to talk to You about Negativity

Michael Newman

CONCORDIA PUBLISHING HOUSE · SAINT LOUIS

Copyright © 2013 Concordia Publishing House
3558 S. Jefferson Avenue, St. Louis, MO 63118-3968
1-800-325-3040 · www.cph.org



Written by Michael Newman



Manufactured in the United States of America

1 2 3 4 5 6 7 8 9 10 22 21 20 19 18 17 16 15 14 13

# Table of CONTENTS


| | |
|---|---|
| Introduction | 4 |
| Topical Prayers | 6 |
| General Prayers | 44 |
| Suggested Scripture Readings | 47 |

A note to the reader: Some of the details in these prayers may not reflect your unique situation. Therefore, we encourage you to adapt them where appropriate to fit your circumstances and spiritual needs.

# Introduction

Chronic negativity. It's like slipping into an old, comfy pair of sweatpants.

We're the first to see the fatal flaw or point out a problem. It's apparent to us what's wrong with this picture, and we feel compelled to draw attention to it. Besides, everyone has a right to an opinion.

It's important to recognize that verbalizing a negative response is a choice that we make and that we are responsible for our words. It's true that things go wrong and that there's room for improvement in almost everything. We can't control what happens in the world or what other people do. The only thing we can truly control is how we react. We can give in to negativity and choose to tear down. Or we can exercise discipline and self-control so we use words that are productive and uplifting. We can decide to be positive.

But habits are hard to break and our sinful human nature constantly works against us. And more than that, Satan wants us to be at odds with the world. He knows us very well and is a master at conflict. He wants us to see only what's wrong. He does not want us to lift one another up. He does not want us to have one little, tiny shred of hope.

We don't have to give in to Satan. Looking for the good in a situation is a choice. The apostle Paul said, "Whatever is true, whatever is honorable, whatever is just, whatever is pure, whatever is lovely, whatever is commendable, if there is any excellence, if there is anything worthy of praise, think about these things" (Philippians 4:8).

Retraining ourselves to respond in constructive ways is possible, but that's only part of the process. Real change requires a transformation that only God can do. Through the work of Jesus Christ on the cross, Satan's destructive ways and our sinful human nature have already been defeated. Through Christ, we are made new. He changes us from hopeless people to sons and daughters of a merciful heavenly Father.

We're not doomed. The news is good! Our future is bright because Jesus shines His light into our lives and throughout the sin-darkened world. Let that joy show through you!

# Shocked

## Dear God,

I had an unusual conversation today. A friend of mine approached me after a meeting and told me in a very gentle way that I have the habit of being the negative voice at every meeting. She said that the people in the group look at me as "Debbie Downer."

I was very surprised at this. Honestly, I was hurt to hear it. But my friend was kind. She was a true friend. She told me that she respected me and cared about me. She even said that my opinions and insights are valuable. But my "glass half empty" perspective and my tendency to be critical of others weren't being received well. She said my negative attitude has been hurting the way people listen to me and receive my input.

My friend then issued an interesting challenge. She challenged me not to speak negatively for thirty days. Then she prayed for me.

Thank You, dear God, for this faithful

friend. I'm not sure what to make of her challenge, but she cared enough to speak the truth to me in a loving way. She reminded me about how much You care for me. You reached into my life through Jesus' sacrifice for me on the cross. Today You reached into my life through a friend. Please give me wisdom and peace to go the way You are directing. I need to know what to do. I know You will lead me.

## Something to think about

Lead me in Your truth and teach me, for You are the God of my salvation; for You I wait all the day long. . . . May integrity and uprightness preserve me, for I wait for You.

Psalm 25:5, 21

# Needing Light

Dear God,

People are driving me crazy! I had an awful day today. No one completed the tasks they were assigned to finish before our meeting at work. Construction workers caused a horrible traffic jam on the way home. And everything was a mess when I got there—I don't have any help around the house.

People seem so careless. I don't sense that anyone cares about what I say. I feel like I can't trust anyone to do anything the way it's supposed to be done. It seems like people are coasting along, not wanting to do the right thing. Life seems hopeless sometimes. It seems like everything is going down the tubes. And no one cares enough to do anything about it. Why can't people get things right?

I confess that I'm frustrated and feeling hopeless. I confess that I'm feeling some self-pity. Maybe this is why my friend talked to me about being negative. Maybe I need to focus on Your blessings instead of everyone's faults. Maybe I need to hear Your Word of hope instead of dwelling on all the hopelessness around me.

I want to do that, dear Lord, but I can't do it alone. Please help me to see and respond to things in a new way. I feel trapped in a dark and dismal place. I know You can free me and give me hope. Please show me Your way of new life and salvation.

### Something to think about

There are many who say, "Who will show us some good? Lift up the light of Your face upon us, O LORD!"

Psalm 4:6

# Grumbling

Dear God,

The sermon on Sunday was about the danger of having a spirit of grumbling. I think You had the pastor preach that sermon just for me. He quoted 1 Corinthians 10:10 and said that grumbling was part of what led to the destruction of the people during the time of Moses.

I think I'm a grumbler. I never thought of myself that way. I don't want to be that way. But some recent experiences have shown me that I tend toward the negative. I find the problem instead of the solution. I'm the pessimist and the doubter. I don't give new ideas a chance. Most of all, I think I miss Your blessings. I miss the good things others might contribute.

Thank You for opening my eyes. Thank You for showing me my need. And please forgive me. I don't want to be a person who steals joy from others. I don't want to be someone who pushes people away. The pastor also gave me hope in his sermon. He quoted 1 Corinthians 10:13: "No temptation has overtaken you that is not common to man. God is faithful, and He will not let you be tempted beyond your ability, but with the temptation He will also provide the way of escape, that you may be able to endure it."

I know You are faithful and gracious, dear Savior. Please lead me out of my negativity.

## Something to think about

Humble yourselves before the Lord, and He will lift you up.

James 4:10 NIV

# Positive?

Dear God,

It may be time to accept the challenge from my friend. I was given a compliment about what I was wearing today. Instead of accepting it with a "thank you," I said something about how I could be thinner and younger and how it could fit better. My friend's puzzled look said it all.

I have to admit that when I'm positive about most things, I'm "positive" something will go wrong or I'm "positive" that I'm not good enough. I may never be the perpetual optimist, but I do need to grow in expressing the trust I have in You and the joy of Your salvation. I need to grow in sharing excitement with others and giving people a chance to try things that aren't my idea.

I've noticed that my negativity is pushing people away from me. They don't want to hear my input. They don't want to be around me. This is not only hurting my feelings, it is hurting my ability to bear witness to You, God.

So, I'm ready. Change me and grow me. I know You love me and You have created me to declare Your praises. You have called me out of darkness and into Your light. Please shape my attitude and spirit to shine Your light over the next thirty days.

### Something to think about

But you are a chosen race, a royal priesthood, a holy nation, a people for His own possession, that you may proclaim the excellencies of Him who called you out of darkness into His marvelous light. Once you were not a people, but now you are God's people; once you had not received mercy, but now you have received mercy.

1 Peter 2:9–10

# Peace

Dear God,

For my first day of not being negative, my friend gave me a devotional book. Today's devotion was about You being the Prince of Peace. I praise You for making peace a reality for my life. You do not give as the world gives. You give what is good. You give peace.

Thank You for that gift. I used that gift today by being calm and listening to others. It's something I hardly ever do. Typically, I will react to people. I even interrupt them. If I hear an idea I don't like, or if I disagree strongly with someone's opinion, I'll jump right in. Today was different. I listened. I let people complete their thoughts and sentences. Today, I didn't offer any immediate responses. I thanked people for their ideas and input.

To be honest, people were a bit confused. I wasn't being the old me. But the only way I could stop the negativity today was to be silent. What surprised me most is that people thanked me for listening. I think they felt respected and cared for. This day was strangely good. I felt less of a burden when the day was over.

Thank You for this new beginning, dear Prince of Peace. You have opened a new door of genuine peace in my life.

## Something to think about

Let your reasonableness be known to everyone. The Lord is at hand; do not be anxious about anything, but in everything by prayer and supplication with thanksgiving let your requests be made known to God. And the peace of God, which surpasses all understanding, will guard your hearts and your minds in Christ Jesus.

Philippians 4:5–7

# Humbled

Dear God,

This new way of expressing myself is not very comfortable for me. I'm biting my tongue and swallowing my pride. But You are helping me. Today I read about Jesus, who humbled Himself—even to death on the cross. There are so many reasons Your Son could have disagreed with Your plan to save us. But even in the face of our negativity and sin, He gave Himself up for us—for me.

Today I didn't constantly disagree with people. I tried to find the good in what they were doing. When my son's bed wasn't made perfectly, I praised him for the fact that he did what I asked. When my co-worker got creative with some customer contacts, I complimented her on her new approach. When my friend ordered her favorite coffee flavor, I didn't criticize it like I usually do. I acknowledged that it is her favorite.

People are looking at me like someone else

has taken over my body, but I am seeing delight in their eyes. My son gave me a hug after I told him he did a good job. My co-worker smiled.

I can see that this new practice is helping my relationships. It is helping me feel whole and happy. It is also showing Your presence in my life in a wonderful way. Thank You for humbly serving me, dear God. And thank You for leading me in the footsteps of Jesus, the most faithful Servant of all.

### Something to think about

The Son of Man came not to be served but to serve, and to give His life as a ransom for many.

Matthew 20:28

# Control

Dear God,

Today I felt afraid of losing control. If I keep quiet or give only affirmation, I feel like I have no ability to have any say in the conversation. If I let something go that I disagree with, I'm afraid that an entire project might crash and burn. If I let my kids do only 80 percent of what they're supposed to, I fret that they may end up taking advantage of me.

I need to understand how to give input without being negative. I need to learn how to be positive while I set boundaries and expectations. This is very difficult.

But I know You sacrificed everything for me. Your sacrifice didn't cause Your plan to crash and burn. Your loving sacrifice accomplished exactly what You desired most. Help me to trust that by sacrificing my negative comments and attitudes, Your plan for my life will be accomplished better. Lead me to speak the truth in a loving and balanced way. Please remove bitterness, sarcasm, and pride from the way I think, communicate, and react. Let this sacrifice renew my relationships and allow me to contribute instead of control, to help create instead of constantly tear down.

## Something to think about

Therefore be imitators of God, as beloved children. And walk in love, as Christ loved us and gave Himself up for us, a fragrant offering and sacrifice to God.

Ephesians 5:1–2

# Distracted

Dear God,

During an important meeting at church, I couldn't hold back. I launched into all the reasons why the proposed fellowship event was going to fail. I was fully back into my negativity mode, and it was only day four of my challenge! After I said my piece in the meeting, I could tell that I sucked all the life out of the room. People were silent. They looked around and decided they would revisit the issue at another time.

I felt like a failure and fool. I felt like a hypocrite. I was doing so well. Now I was acting like the "old me."

But You rescued me. After a break in the meeting, I was able to apologize for my negativity, affirm some positive points of the proposal, and thank everyone for letting me serve with them in such an important ministry. I never would have done that before, but You took me by the hand and lifted me up out of my own failure.

Thank You for giving me a second chance. With a simple apology, You allowed me to continue on the path of trusting in You and showing Your mercy.

## Something to think about

But when [Peter] saw the wind, he was afraid, and beginning to sink he cried out, "Lord, save me." Jesus immediately reached out His hand and took hold of him, saying to him, "O you of little faith, why did you doubt?"

Matthew 14:30–31

# Rest

Dear God,

Today is a new day. It is the day You have made. I will rejoice and be glad in it.

Those are the powerful words from Psalm 118:24 I read in my devotion today. Rejoicing and being glad haven't been a big part of my life lately. But I'm getting more acquainted with those two actions in recent days. I am rejoicing as I see the blessings You have placed in my life. For some reason, I only saw the deficiencies in the past. I'm being glad about the uniqueness of people and the variety of ideas I encounter.

This is not always easy. Honestly, it makes me uncomfortable. I like things to be safe. Risk scares me. Getting out of my comfort zone feels risky to me. When I am confronted with what seems to be an unnecessary risk, I push back. My pushes are usually in some form of negativity.

Thank You for showing me that I don't have

to be the watchdog and protector. I can relax, trust in You, and rest in the fact that You are taking care of things. I can let ideas play out. I can experiment with some new ways of doing things and all will not be lost.

You have given me freedom that I did not have before, dear God. Thank You for that. Thank You for leading me away from constant negativity. Most of all, thank You for letting me rest in You as I travel this unfamiliar path.

## Something to think about

Come to Me, all who labor and are heavy laden, and I will give you rest. Take My yoke upon you, and learn from Me, for I am gentle and lowly in heart, and you will find rest for your souls.

Matthew 11:28–29

# Encouragement

Dear God,

Today's devotion was about a man named Barnabas. His name means "son of encouragement." He helped share the Good News of Jesus' death and resurrection with people who lived in a city called Antioch. They were the first people who were called Christians.

I think I like Barnabas. I would like to be a person of encouragement too.

My normal mode of operation was to force my input into a conversation or to play the "devil's advocate" when evaluating any idea. I felt it was my role to find everything wrong with everything. But now I see how destructive that is. Like Barnabas, I can be heard, I can teach, and I can share ideas as an encourager instead of as a cynic or critic. This is what I would like to practice.

You have encouraged me with Your love, dear Savior. You have given me a friend who cared enough to speak the truth to me in a kind way. You have encouraged me through Your Word. You have encouraged me by saving me. Thank You.

Please give me confidence that people will hear me when I speak positively and constructively. Please help me to speak in a way that lifts people up—even when I offer a critique. Please shape me in my thoughts, actions, and words to be a person of encouragement.

## Something to think about

For God has not destined us for wrath, but to obtain salvation through our Lord Jesus Christ, who died for us so that whether we are awake or asleep we might live with Him. Therefore encourage one another and build one another up, just as you are doing.

1 Thessalonians 5:9–11

# Kindness

Dear God,

During the course of this journey out of negativity, I've realized that I'm not the only one struggling with the issue. Some people are outwardly negative, offering criticisms freely and being naysayers about almost everything. It's easy to spot outward negativity. I confess that I have been one of those people. I could always find something wrong.

But there are some people who live in quiet and hidden negativity. They criticize themselves or live in doubt and depression, having virtually no hope. As I've journeyed through taking a hard look at my own negativity, I've developed a heart for people who are trapped by this silent oppressor. That's why I decided to try to give a compliment or affirmation to as many people as possible today.

This practice really changed my focus. Instead of getting stuck on issues that bothered me, I began to look for people who needed encouragement. My "inner Barnabas" started to come out as I tried to notice the good people were doing and the blessings people embodied. I let my co-worker know that I admire how neat and orderly her desk is. I told my husband that he is good at paying the bills. I told my son that I like his laugh.

To be honest, it was fun to find ways to affirm people. It helps keep my mind off the negative. This wasn't my idea, God. You provided it through the kindness of Your Word. I am now enjoying passing along Your kindness.

### Something to think about

Anxiety in a man's heart weighs him down, but a good word makes him glad.

Proverbs 12:25

# Prayer

## Dear God,

The devotion for the day helped me in my new life of being more positive. The verse I read was from James 1:19: "Know this, my beloved brothers: let every person be quick to hear, [and] slow to speak."

Thank You for opening my ears to hear Your Word of grace and love in my life. You have been patient with me. You have reached into my life to grow me. You are shaping me into a better witness of Your love and care. Thank You for taking Your time with me.

I want to follow You by taking my time with others. Instead of jumping into a discussion, help me listen well. Help me see below the surface of the conversation so I can consider a person's heart and motivations. Help me pause to think before I speak. Most of all, lead me to ask You for Your wisdom instead of relying on my own. You have given me the gift of prayer.

Lead me to lift up my prayers to You before I speak. Help me to watch and listen for Your leadership so that Your will may be done and Your voice may be heard.

You are good, O God. You are trustworthy. I know You are faithful to answer me.

## Something to think about

But as for me, my prayer is to You, O LORD. At an acceptable time, O God, in the abundance of Your steadfast love answer me in Your saving faithfulness.

Psalm 69:13

# Problems

## Dear God,

You are compassionate and gracious, slow to anger, and abounding in love. You are a faithful Savior. You came to seek and save me through Jesus, Your Son.

Thank You for reconditioning my heart, for gently putting my pride and arrogance to death, and for growing the fruit of the Holy Spirit in me. Patience, peace, kindness, and self-control are blessings from You.

You have also opened my eyes to see life differently and to respond to others differently. I see Your blessings. I am learning to appreciate people's perspectives and practices. We're all different. I realize that everyone doesn't have to think like me or be like me.

I am learning how to disagree with people in a more constructive way. My husband was doing a project at home in what I thought was a dangerous way. In my past way of doing things, I would have been critical and bossy.

This time around, I thanked him for what he was doing, let him know that I wanted him to be safe because I cared about him, and asked if he could take steps that wouldn't cause him to be hurt. Instead of fighting about it, we had a constructive conversation. It went very well.

Battling negativity takes thought, prayer, and effort, but I can see that it fosters Your love and brings honor to You.

Thank You for Your gracious way of dealing with problems.

## Something to think about

A soft answer turns away wrath, but a harsh word stirs up anger.

Proverbs 15:1

# Wisdom

## Dear God,

Today I am asking You for wisdom. I need to know how to determine if my thoughts are honest and constructive or if I am being negative and critical. My friend is helping me with some accountability, but I need Your wisdom from moment to moment. Some of my thoughts are immediately critical. My outlook very easily veers toward pessimism. There are times I consider it foolish and unreasonable to be positive about something.

Please guide me. Sometimes one of my attempts at humor is really a negative and hurtful comment. At other times I try to take the lead by becoming forceful and abrasive to others. Because I can be naturally negative, I need You to help me learn how to speak the truth in love. I need Your wisdom to help me move forward with genuine critiques at the proper times.

You sent Your Son who was oppressed

and afflicted but didn't open His mouth with critical words. Fill me with the Spirit of Jesus as You walk with me in the new life You have given me.

## Something to think about

You desired faithfulness even in the womb; You taught me wisdom in that secret place.

Psalm 51:6 NIV

# The Big Picture

Dear God,

One thing You've made very clear in this journey is that life is not all about me.

I don't know if I ever really thought it was, but I lived like it. I wanted my ideas to be adopted, my ways to be followed, and my opinions to be validated. I wanted to be right all the time. It made me feel worthwhile and valued.

But Your Word has shown me that Your love is what I really need. You have shown through the sacrifice of Your Son that I am valued. I am precious in Your sight.

Now Your love has given me freedom. I can now affirm others and put others before me. Instead of feeling threatened, I can celebrate new ideas and welcome the uniqueness of others. As I do this, I can trust that You will sort out the details—even using me at times to bring constructive input.

Thank You for lifting me up with Your

grace. It's been over a week and a half in my no-negativity challenge. People are noticing. My relationships are becoming healthier. I don't see fear and dread in people's eyes when I walk into a room. Above all, Your love is shining through me more than it ever did.

I praise You, O Lord, for the big picture You graciously provide.

## Something to think about

Beloved, let us love one another, for love is from God, and whoever loves has been born of God and knows God.

1 John 4:7

# Leadership

Dear God,

Jesus' words, "Follow Me," reach my heart and soul these days. From grumbling, complaining, and seeing the worst in things, He calls me to follow Him in a pathway of grace and new life. He leads me in the path of righteousness and to streams of living water. Through Jesus' faithful work, I have been made brand new. Thank You so much for this blessing, dear Lord.

You've also shown me that my journey away from negativity is a journey of outreach to others. I see that my practice of being positive is really a practice of positive Christian leadership. It sets an example of faith for young and old. It calls people away from cynicism and arrogance. It directs people to an attitude of faith and a spirit of trust in You.

Thank You for using me as an instrument in Your hand, O God. You allow me to reflect Your faithfulness to the people around me. I didn't understand this before, but now I realize that my words and attitudes bear witness to who You are and to the Good News You give us every day.

Thank You for rescuing me from the dark place of pessimism and gloom. Thank You for the honor of being someone who is now Your servant who shares Your hope in a hopeless world.

## Something to think about

Let us hold fast the confession of our hope without wavering, for He who promised is faithful. And let us consider how to stir up one another to love and good works.

Hebrews 10:23–24

# Transformation

Dear God,

It's been almost two weeks in my no-negativity challenge. I like what You are doing in my life. I praise You for Your gracious help and for the way You've reshaped my outlook. Speaking constructively and positively is becoming a good habit. It is replacing my old way of life.

I take no credit for this transformation. Your Word has been a powerful tool that continues to change me. The devotion book my friend gave me has been a wonderful gift.

People have helped me, too. My pastor has been very supportive with his prayers, teaching, and preaching. He has also encouraged me in conversations and with accountability. My friend has been a key factor in my new life. She cared about me enough to tell me the truth. She still walks with me and encourages me every day.

Thank You for surrounding me with open doors and trustworthy resources. I didn't know how much I needed to change, but now You have created in me the desire to grow and reflect Your positive, constructive, and life-building character. You've also renewed my sense of joy and hope in life.

I give You glory and praise, dear God, for a new and transformed life by Your grace.

## Something to think about

And He died for all, that those who live might no longer live for themselves but for Him who for their sake died and was raised. From now on, therefore, we regard no one according to the flesh. Even though we once regarded Christ according to the flesh, we regard Him thus no longer. Therefore, if anyone is in Christ, he is a new creation. The old has passed away; behold, the new has come.

2 Corinthians 5:15–17

# Good Hands

Dear God,

You have slowed me down and opened my eyes to see others and myself in a way that I have never experienced.

When I look at myself, I see a sinner who stumbles so easily, who defaults to the negative, who becomes afraid, and who reacts defensively. I see someone who, left alone, would become a hopeless cynic.

But now I see someone different. I see a new creation, a baptized and redeemed child of God who is loved and cherished, a person bought by the blood of Jesus, now raised up to display His hope and life.

You have given me a new heart, a new life, and a new perspective.

When I look at others, I realize I used to see people who interrupted me and annoyed me. I saw fault-filled people who made poor judgments and bad decisions.

But now I see Your children. I see people

for whom You gave Your Son. I see people who have gifts and perspectives that can help show Your Good News in unique and wonderful ways.

Thank You, O Lord, for slowing me down, renewing my heart, adjusting my perspective, and using me as Your servant. Thank You for Your salvation. I am in Your good hands.

## Something to think about

Create in me a clean heart, O God, and renew a right spirit within me. Cast me not away from Your presence, and take not Your Holy Spirit from me. Restore to me the joy of Your salvation, and uphold me with a willing spirit.

Psalm 51:10–12

# A New Day

## Dear God,

Today is a new day. It is a gift from You. You have washed away my sins and have given me a new beginning today. Thank You.

It's been just over two weeks in my journey away from negativity. I know I will never eliminate negativity from my life. I am a sinner, and I fail so easily. But I do know that You free me from being enslaved to negativity. The dark and dreary walk of life that leads only to death has been destroyed through Christ's death and resurrection. Now I have eternal hope that crushes every reason to be cynical and pessimistic. My hope is in You.

You also live in me. Having Your mind and Your Spirit in me allows me to see life differently and to see people differently. It is a joy to encounter others with the anticipation of what You have planned rather than with my own dread of handling life my way.

During this time of prayer, You have shown

me that my goal is to express Christ who lives in me, not the ME who lives in me.

You have accomplished so much for me, dear Savior. Through Your Word and through the presence of Jesus in Holy Communion, You have made Your home in my life. Keep lifting me up as Your positive and hope-filled servant who brings Your wisdom, Your love, and Your encouragement to each person and each situation on each new and blessed day.

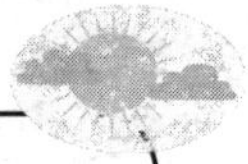

## Something to think about

I have been crucified with Christ. It is no longer I who live, but Christ who lives in me. And the life I now live in the flesh I live by faith in the Son of God, who loved me and gave Himself for me.

Galatians 2:20

# General Prayers

## LORD'S PRAYER

Our Father, who art in heaven, hallowed be Thy name, Thy kingdom come, Thy will be done on earth as it is in heaven. Give us this day our daily bread; and forgive us our trespasses as we forgive those who trespass against us; and lead us not into temptation, but deliver us from evil. For Thine is the kingdom and the power and the glory forever and ever. Amen.

## MORNING PRAYER

I thank You, my heavenly Father, through Jesus Christ, Your dear Son, that You have kept me this night from all harm and danger; and I pray that You would keep me this day also from sin and every evil, that all my doings and life may please You. For into Your hands I commend myself, my body and soul, and all things. Let Your holy angel be with me, that the evil foe may have no power over me. Amen. (Martin Luther)

# EVENING PRAYER

I thank You, my heavenly Father, through Jesus Christ, Your dear Son, that You have graciously kept me this day; and I pray that You would forgive me all my sins where I have done wrong, and graciously keep me this night. For into Your hands I commend myself, my body and soul, and all things. Let Your holy angel be with me, that the evil foe may have no power over me. Amen. (Martin Luther)

# FOR STEADFAST FAITH

Dear Savior, You have brought me safely to this day. I did not know Your plan for me—what troubles and what joys would be part of my day. Lord, grant that I may look back at all the things that You have provided and recognize the good You have done for me. Let me view the successes of each day as encouragements and as undeserved gifts coming from Your gracious hands. Let me accept the pains and perplexities as reminders, chastening, and directions toward repentance and improvement. Keep me steadfast in faith, abundant in service, warm in love, and unceasing in prayer. You have redeemed me, my great God and Savior; I am Yours. Amen. (adapted from *LBP*, p. 21)

## FOR FORGIVENESS

Lord Jesus Christ, You have provided a sacrifice for all our sins and opened again for us the gates of paradise, which were closed to us on account of our transgressions. Through Your loving kindness, I have not been left in the ruins of my sin; You have saved me by Your Word, washed me clean in Holy Baptism, and declared that I am a child of Your grace. And though I walk the way of Your commandments with halting steps, You daily forgive all my sins. With a grateful heart I look to You. Grant that I may ever and always accept the mysteries of Your Word and the blessings that come to me through the means of grace. Amen. (adapted from *LBP*, p. 139)

# Suggested Scripture Readings

This is the day that the LORD has made; let us rejoice and be glad in it.

Psalm 118:24

Finally, brothers, whatever is true, whatever is honorable, whatever is just, whatever is pure, whatever is lovely, whatever is commendable, if there is any excellence, if there is anything worthy of praise, think about these things.

Philippians 4:8

Let all bitterness and wrath and anger and clamor and slander be put away from you, along with all malice. Be kind to one another, tenderhearted, forgiving one another, as God in Christ forgave you.

Ephesians 4:31–32

Do not repay evil for evil or reviling for reviling, but on the contrary, bless, for to this you were called, that you may obtain a blessing.

1 Peter 3:9

So, whether you eat or drink, or whatever you do, do all to the glory of God.

1 Corinthians 10:31

And above all these put on love, which binds everything together in perfect harmony. And let the peace of Christ rule in your hearts, to which indeed you were called in one body. And be thankful. Let the word of Christ dwell in you richly, teaching and admonishing one another in all wisdom, singing psalms and hymns and spiritual songs, with thankfulness in your hearts to God.

Colossians 3:14–16

Let the words of my mouth and the meditation of my heart be acceptable in Your sight, O Lord, my rock and my redeemer.

Psalm 19:14